Just mini Cocktails

cocktails & party drinks

Fun & Exciting Cocktail Recipes

for casual entertaining and tasting parties

by Robert Zollweg

Designed and written by Robert Zollweg
Photography by Rick Luettke, www.luettkestudio.com
Graphics by Gary Raschke and Robert Zollweg
Art Direction by Gary Raschke

Library of Congress Cataloging-in-Publication Data:

Just mini Cocktails,
Cocktails and Party Drinks
by Robert Zollweg

www.zollwegart.com

ISBN 978-0-615-49813-3

Printed in the United States of America
By: R. R. Donnelley and Company

I'd like to dedicate this cookbook to

John and Ann Meier

for their leadership, passion, support, friendship
and understanding to me and to our great company

To my mother, Virginia, my kids, Christopher and Rhonda
and all their children
Kaylie, Andrew, Bret, Morgan and Korrin
Steve Tester, Elaine and Tom Bender, Richard and Sandra Zollweg
Judy and Carl Sims, all their families
and to Annie.

There are so many people to thank for making this cookbook a reality.

Gary Raschke, I could not have made it happen without his help,
and Bill Muzzillo's great literary skills.
Karen Barentzen, Beth Baroncini, Cathie Logan, Tom Fratantuono,
Denise Grigg, Kelly Kelley, Roger Williams, Jeff Joyce, Serena Williams,
Jessica Adler, Gina Baccari, Vicki Richardson, Amy Lewarchik, Greg Pax,
Brooks Clayton, Natalie Brunner, Sandy Shultz, Brionna Richmond, Melissa Fleig,
Fran Breitner, Ericka Sabo, Rosie Jordan and Brenda Bennett.

Cindy Kretzinger for your inspiration and friendship

Nancy, Michael, Claudia, Nicole and Lisa

Libbey Glass for giving me the opportunity to do what I enjoy doing.

Table of Contents

Introduction 8 - 9

Glassware, Preparation and Servings 10 - 19

Martinis and Margaritas 20 - 43

Tropical Cocktails 44 - 61

Classic Cocktails 62 - 77

Party Punches 78 - 87

Smoothies and Non Alcoholic Cocktails 88 - 103

Coffees, Teas and Hot Chocolates 104 - 117

Beer and Wine Tastings 118 - 123

Index 124 - 125

Introduction

Just mini Cocktails is a trendy way to serve ordinary cocktails at your next party or get together but adding a unique twist by serving them in little mini glasses for tastings or samplings. I've adapted many of my favorite cocktail recipes to fit into these little glass containers just because they look so darn cool. They make for a fabulous presentation and, by the way, they look and taste great and are easy as can be to prepare.

Just mini Cocktails is also about presentation. Most of the cocktail recipes are pretty standard, but I've added little nuances to spice them up and add a little pizzazz. Grouping them together is what tasting cocktails is all about. I will make several different flavors of the same cocktail in a small pitcher and let my guests sample small tastings of each. This way they can experiment and try things they haven't had before.

The whole idea behind just tastings started a few years ago at the National Restaurant Show in Chicago. Restaurants were seeing an increase in popularity with serving desserts, appetizers, soups and cocktails in small containers. As a result, they started developing and serving these items off their menus in petite or taster versions. To make them special and more exciting, they found small glass and ceramic containers to show off their new creations. **Just mini Cocktails** is a natural extention. They are usually served in multiples with a variety of different cocktails to choose from. I felt this was something today's consumers would love and were missing in the marketplace, especially when it came to home entertaining. Most of the following mini cocktail recipes are pretty quick and simple to make. So I've created this collection of my favorite cocktail recipes that will hopefully make your next cocktail party a huge success.

I like to serve my mini cocktails in 3-4 oz glasses so all my guests can try as many different cocktails as they like. Most of my guests sample them all.

You can adapt almost any cocktail recipe to mini cocktails. Mix them any way you like. Just serve them in little glasses along with your favorite appetizers.

Displaying mini cocktails is what is most important and key to a festive party or get together. Using a variety of different servers and tiered trays help make this a more fashionable and trendy presentation. See photos on the following pages for a few creative ideas. These presentations are great for special parties, big birthdays (30, 40, 50, etc.) for Super Bowl or the Oscars, to name a few. You will look very professional and trendy and your guests will love to come over to your house.

I hope you enjoy these wonderful **Just mini Cocktails** as much as I have enjoyed creating them. I have been using them a lot lately. They are so easy to put together. Making a variety of appetizers and desserts to go along with the cocktails for a tasting party is just so much fun and will make your party a lot more interesting.

Working in the tabletop industry has been very rewarding and it is where I have learned so much about entertaining. I love to entertain and I hope that **Just mini Cocktails** will be a great way for you to turn your next festive occasion, cocktail or tasting party into something really special.

Enjoy !   Robert

Glassware

■

Preparation & Garnishes

■

Serving Presentations

The following pages will show you some wonderful glass items for serving tasting cocktails. There are many more different styles in the marketplace that will work just as well. I'll give you a few easy ideas on the preparation and garnishing of the mini tasting cocktails and some tips on presentation to make this tasting party a fun and festive occasion for you and your guests.

Remember the golden rule: Always make your guests feel at home. Always have food and beverages that are common to your guests' tastes. Sometimes you can go just a little beyond to experiment, but not too far. They need to feel comfortable and you need to be relaxed and at ease for your enjoyment, too. Parties should not be stressful, so keep it simple and casual. These cocktail recipes, along with your favorite tasting appetizers, will help guarantee a successful tasting party. Enjoy !

Glassware

On the following two pages are some of the glass containers I use to show off these fabulous tasting cocktails. There are so many wonderful pieces of glass that can be used to serve any of these tasting cocktails. Use your imagination. Mix it up. Who's to say martinis need to be served in a martini glass? Try a cordial or rocks glass. A tall shooter glasses make a wonderful container for any cold cocktail.

Many of your favorite cocktail recipes can be made into mini tasting cocktails. If you can make a single portion, you can easily make multiple portions. I like to make tasting cocktails in a small glass pitcher for martini, margaritas, pina coladas, etc. Serving them in mini glasses for smaller portions for tasting is what this cookbook is all about.

Be creative! There are so many cool glasses for mini cocktails. The containers I have used in this publication can be purchased from various area retailers.

These mini cocktail presentations are just what you need for a exciting cocktail tasting party.

Preparation and Tools

To have a successful cocktail tasting party, you will need several small 30-50 ounce glass pitchers, a couple of ice buckets and several martini shakers for mixing the cocktails along with a variety of mini glassware for serving these tasting cocktails. The photographs on the following pages will explain this a little more clearly.

A blender is nice to have, especially when you are making larger quantities of frozen or frothy cocktails. A tall sleek glass pitcher is wonderful for flavored martinis and other classic cocktails. When making fruit smoothies, you can add almost any fruit or combination of fruit to the mixture. Be creative and it will almost always come out fabulous.

Simple Syrup: To make simple syrup, bring 1 cup sugar and 1/2 cup water to a boil until sugar is completely dissolved, stir. Let cool and refrigerate until ready to use.

14

Garnishes

Garnishing for tasting party cocktails is important because this is what adds the flair and pizzazz to the cocktail. Most are very simple but a few get a little more creative. Keep it as simple or as complicated as you are comfortable with. Oranges, limes and lemons make ideal garnishes for most cocktails.

Serving Presentations

When I'm entertaining at home, I use a variety of mini cocktails and appetizers on different platters and servers. Use your favorite tasting appetizers to compliment your mini tasting cocktails. This photo shows a simple way to serve several different tasting cocktails on a buffet table at home. Sometimes I combine the tasting cocktails with tasting appetizers and desserts or I separate them on different tables. It is up to you to decide how much space you have or how elaborate you want to get. Either way, your guests will love the festive and unique presentation.

Try having a chocolate tasting party with various chocolate mini desserts and complimenting wine or liquors. It's a delicious combination your guests will love and enjoy.

Here is a fun idea. Set up a hot beverage station in your kitchen so it is all ready to go after your have finished dinner or an evening of cards or games. Hot chocolate, flavored teas and wonderful coffees are great when served in little coffee mugs or Irish coffee glasses. It's pretty simple to do and relatively inexpensive.

Here's an example of a wine tasting buffet using mini wine tasters and appetizers. This would be a great buffet idea for your guests right before they leave for a movie or concert, something light and festive. There are many wonderful cheeses that can be purchased to compliment your favorite red or white wines. Ask your local grocer or someone in the wine department.

This photo shows an example of a cocktail tasting party that offers almost everything for everyone's tastes. I've used several cocktail shakers for different flavors of martinis and two small glass pitchers for serving sangria and mojitos. I also use wine chillers for different white wines and a galvanized tub for chilling the craft brew specialty beers. But what is most important is having a variety of mini glasses for serving each kind of the tasting cocktail. Mini cocktail glasses are important because you want your guests to be able to sample all the different ones you are offering. Don't forget to add another table of **Just Tasting** appetizers, soups and salads to compliment your tasting cocktails. Serving food is always important when serving alcoholic beverages, as you do not want your guests to drink on an empty stomach.

Here is an example of some different filled mini glasses to give you some ideas for a more unusual presentation.

Here is an example of a beer tasting party. These are not really cocktails, but specialty and craft beers are very popular. Serve specialty beers along with tasting cocktails. I use a galvanized tub filled with ice to chill the beer. You can also use a large serving bowl or plastic container. Having several different kinds or styles of craft beers is what tasting is all about and a lot more interesting. Make sure you start your beer tasting evening with lighter beers like a pilsner and finish off the evening with darker more full bodied beers like porters or stouts. Lighter beers should be served cold and darker beers slightly chilled or even room temperature. Serve them along with some **Just Tasting** appetizers.

Martinis and Margaritas

Cosmopolitan

The Cosmopolitan is a very sexy and delicious cocktail. It can be served in almost any small stemmed glass. This recipe calls for it to be shakened. But it can also be mixed in a small glass pitcher and stirred.

You will need a 24 oz metal cocktail shaker. This will make enough to fill 8 -10 small 3 oz mini martini glasses.

6 oz Absolut Citron Vodka
1-1/2 oz Roses lime juice
3 oz Cointreau
3 oz cranberry juice
1 oz simple syrup (page 14)
1 cup of crushed ice
Several orange twists or lime wedges for garnish (one for each glass)

Fill a cocktail shaker with ice, add the ingredients and shake until ice cold (about 15 seconds). Pour gently into the mini martini glasses and garnish with a orange twist. Arrange on a platter or tray along with your favorite appetizers and serve. Enjoy !

Non Alcoholic Cosmopolitan

Use the same recipe as above but substitute the vodka or gin with a lemon lime soda and use a little extra lime juice. Stir instead of shake. Serve and Enjoy !

Chocolate Martini

Chocolate martinis are especially delicious when served at a mini dessert buffet. They can be served in almost any small stemmed glasses. This recipe calls for the martini to be shakened. But it can also be mixed in a small glass pitcher and stirred.

You will need a 24oz cocktail shaker. This recipe will make enough to fill 8 -10 small 3oz mini martini glasses.

6 oz vodka
4 oz white cream de cocoa
2 oz cream or half and half
Several chocolate kisses (one for each glass)
A couple of ounces of shaved chocolate for garnish

Fill a cocktail shaker with ice, add the vodka, cream and cream de cocoa and shake until ice cold, about 15 seconds. Place a chocolate kiss in the bottom of each glass. Gently pour into each mini martini glasses and garnish with some chocolate shavings. Arrange on a serving tray along with your favorite appetizers. Serve and Enjoy !

Mocha Chocolate Martini

Follow the recipe from above but add 6 ounces of dark rich coffee to the ingredients before shaking. Garnish with a chocolate kiss and chocolate shavings. Serve and Enjoy !

Appletini

Green Apple martinis or appletinis, as they are commonly called, are especially delicious when served with several thinly sliced Granny Smith apples. They can be served in almost any small stemmed glass. This recipe calls for the Appletini to be shakened. But it can also be mixed in a small glass pitcher and stirred.

You will need a 24oz cocktail shaker. This recipe will make enough to fill 8 -10 small 3oz mini martini glasses

6 oz vodka
3 oz Midori
3 oz apple schnapps
1 tbsp simple syrup (page 14)
10 thinly sliced Granny Smith apples for garnish, optional

Fill a cocktail shaker half full of ice, add the ingredients and shake until ice cold, about 15 seconds. Pour gently into the mini martini glasses and garnish with an apple slice. Arrange on a platter or tray. Serve along with your favorite appetizers. Enjoy !

Lemontini

The lemon martini (or Lemontini) is especially delicious when served with your favorite lemon dessert. It can be served in almost any small stemmed glass. This recipe calls for it to be shakened. But it can also be mixed in a small glass pitcher and stirred.

You will need a 24oz cocktail shaker. This recipe will make enough to fill 8 -10 small 3oz mini martini glasses

6 oz citron vodka
2 oz Grand Marnier, Triple Sec or Cointreau
3 oz fresh lemon juice
1 oz simple syrup (page 14)
splash of lime juice
8 -10 lemon twists or wedges

Fill a cocktail shaker with ice, add the ingredients and shake until ice cold, about 15 seconds. Pour gently into the mini martini glasses and garnish with a lemon twist or wedge. Arrange on a platter or tray. Serve along with your favorite appetizers. Enjoy !

Pineapple Martini

Follow the recipe from above but substitute pineapple juice and pineapple wedges. Omit the simple syrup. Enjoy !

Classic Martini (ala Marlene Dietrich)

The classic martini has been around since the early 20th century. It has been shakened, stirred and flavored and has had more things added to the simple combination of gin and vermouth than you can imagine. But most of all, it's a classic. Gin, never vodka, was what all the stars of the first talking films use to say. But today, vodka is the beverage of choice. It can be served in almost any small stemmed glass. This recipe calls for it to be shaken. But it can also be mixed in a small glass pitcher and stirred.

You will need a 24oz cocktail shaker. This recipe will make enough to fill 8 -10 small 3oz mini martini glasses

12 oz of an expensive gin (you can use vodka)
2 oz vermouth
20 -24 green olives for garnish, 2-3 per toothpick

Fill a cocktail shaker with ice, add the ingredients and shake until ice cold, about 15 seconds. Pour gently into the chilled mini martini glasses and garnish with several green olives. Arrange on a platter or tray. Serve along with your favorite appetizers. Enjoy !

Dirty Dame Martini

This martini is like the classic from above but with an added contemporary twist of olive juice and blue cheese stuffed olives. The only difference is you add 1 oz of green olive juice. Follow directions from above and Enjoy !

Mojotini

The Mojotini is a new combination of a classic martini and a Cuban Mojito. It is especially delicious when served in the summer with lots of ice. It can be served in almost any small stemmed martini glass. This recipe calls for it to be shakened. But I like to make Mojotinis in a pitcher and serve them to all my friends on the patio at the lake.

You will need a 24oz cocktail shaker. This recipe will make enough to fill 8 -10 small 3oz mini martini glasses

6 oz citron vodka
2 oz Cointreau or Triple Sec
3 oz fresh lime juice
1 oz simple syrup, a little more or less, depending on your sweetness level (page 14)
20 - 24 fresh mint leaves, put aside 8-10 for garnish
8 -10 lime wedges, one for each glass

Fill a cocktail shaker with ice, add the first five ingredients and shake until ice cold, about 15 seconds. Pour gently into the chilled mini martini glasses and garnish with a lime wedge and a couple of mint leaves.

When making the Mojotini in a pitcher, crush a few mint leaves in the bottom of the pitcher with some lime juice and simple syrup. Add the rest of the ingredients along with some ice and stir.

Arrange on a platter or tray. Serve along with one of your favorite guacamole appetizers. Enjoy !

Cotton Candy Martini

This martini is especially unique because you will think you are drinking liquid cotton candy. My associate, Fran Breitner, came up with the name. It is so fitting for this unique martini. It can be served in almost any small stemmed glass. This recipe calls for it to be shakened. But it can also be mixed in a small glass pitcher and stirred.

You will need a 24oz cocktail shaker. This recipe will make enough to fill 8 -10 small 3oz mini martini glasses

6 oz vodka
3 oz Triple Sec or Cointreau
5 oz Blue Raspberry MIx
1 oz simple syrup (see page14)
20 or so Maraschino cherries or raspberries, 2-3 per toothpick

Fill a cocktail shaker with ice, add the first four ingredients and shake until ice cold, about 15 seconds. Pour gently into the mini martini glasses and garnish with the maraschino cherries. Arrange the mini martini glasses on a platter or tray. Serve along with your favorite appetizers. Enjoy !

Pomegranate Martini

Pomegranate martinis are refreshingly unique and very trendy. They can be served in almost any small stemmed glass. This recipe calls for the martini to be shakened. But it can also be mixed in a small glass pitcher and stirred.

You will need a 24oz cocktail shaker. This recipe will make enough to fill 8 -10 small 3oz mini martini glasses

6 oz citrus vodka
2 oz lemon juice
2 oz pomegranate juice mix
3 oz simple syrup (page 14)
10 -12 orange twists or some raspberries for garnish

Fill a cocktail shaker with ice, add the first four ingredients and shake until ice cold, about 15 seconds. Pour gently into the mini martini glasses and garnish with a orange twist. Arrange on a platter or tray. Serve along with your favorite appetizers. Enjoy !

The Classic Margarita

This classic margarita is refreshing but traditional with a new twist. I borrowed it from one of my best friends, Elaine Bender. It can be served in almost any small stemmed or small rocks glass. It is best made with a blender but a large glass pitcher will work especially when you need to make a lot for a large party or get together.

You will need a blender or large 50-60 oz glass pitcher. This recipe will make enough to fill 12 -15 small 3oz mini rocks glasses or any mini cocktail glass. The key here is size or ounces of the can of frozen limeade.

1 can frozen limeade concentrate
1 can of tequila
1 can filled with ice cubes and then filled with water
1/3 can of orange juice

10 -12 lime wedges for garnish
Lime wedge and some kosher or sea salt for coating the rim

Start with a blender and put in the can of frozen limeade concentrate. Use this can for a measuring tool. Fill the can with tequila and add to limeade in blender. Add the can of ice and water. Add the 1/3 can of orange juice. Blend on high until smooth and frothy.

Rub the rim of each glass with a lime wedge and carefully dip the rim of each glass into the salt. Pour gently into any of your favorite glasses and garnish with a lime wedge. Arrange on a platter or tray. Serve along with your favorite Mexican appetizers.

This can also be made ahead of time and stored in the freezer. Enjoy !

Citrus Orange Margarita

This margarita has an added citrus twist that makes it especially tasty and refreshing. It can be served in almost any small stemmed or rock glass. I use a blender to make this citrus margarita smooth and frothy.

You will need a blender or a small glass 40-50 oz pitcher for serving. This recipe will make enough to fill 10 -12 small 3oz stem or rocks glasses

12 oz gold tequila
6 oz Triple Sec
12 oz orange juice
1 whole orange, chunked and seeds removed
1/4 cup sugar
2 cups of crushed ice

10 -12 lime or orange slices for garnish
An orange wedge and some granulated sugar for coating the rim for garnish

In your blender, add the first five ingredients and the crushed ice. Blend on high until smooth and frothy. Rub the rim of each glass with an orange wedge and carefully dip the rim of each glass into the sugar. Carefully pour into any of your favorite glasses and garnish with a lime or orange wedge. Arrange on a platter or tray. Or you can fill a glass pitcher with the citrus margarita and let your guests help themselves. Serve along with your favorite Mexican or Caribbean appetizers. Enjoy !

Strawberry Margarita

This is one of my favorite flavored margaritas. It is so refreshing and can be made with almost any fresh or frozen type of berry. I like to use fresh strawberries in the summer. It adds so much flavor. I serve it in these small cocktail glasses when I want to serve a variety of different mini cocktails. I use a blender to get a frozen frothy type of cocktail. But it can also be mixed in a small glass pitcher and stirred.

This will make enough to fill 8 -10 small 3oz mini cocktail glasses

12 oz tequila
6 oz Triple Sec
4 oz fresh lime juice
1 cup fresh or frozen strawberries (try using raspberries or black berries)
2 cups crushed ice

8 -10 fresh strawberries for garnish
One strawberry or lime wedge and some granulated sugar for coating the rim

In a blender, add the first five ingredients and blend until frothy. Rub the rim of the cocktail glass with the lime or strawberry. Then dip the rim of the glass into a saucer of granulated sugar. Fill the glasses with the frozen mixture, garnish with a slice of fresh fruit and arrange on a tray for serving or pour the mixture in a pitcher and let your guests serve themselves. Serve along with your favorite Mexican appetizers. Enjoy !

Tropical Cocktails

Mojito Mojito (the original Cuban Cocktail)

The Mojito originated in Havana, Cuba in the early 1950's, using fresh mint and native rum. It has quickly become an American classic. I always make it in a pitcher because one cocktail is never enough for all my friends at the beach. Fresh mint is sometimes hard to find during the winter months but look hard and you can find it at various gourmet grocery stores. I like serving mojitos in small mini zombie glasses or tall skinny cordial glasses for a unique and festive presentation.

You will need a small 40-50 oz glass pitcher. This recipe will make enough to fill 8 -10 mini zombie or cocktail glasses.

10 oz light rum
20 fresh mint leaves
4 tbsp sugar
crushed ice
1 lime, chunked

4 oz orange liqueur or Triple Sec
4 oz lime juice
16 oz lemon lime soda
10 -12 lime slices for garnish

Muddle or crush the fresh mint, lime chunks, sugar and lime juice in the bottom of the small glass pitcher. Add the rum, orange liqueur and lemon lime soda. Add the crushed ice and stir. Serve on a tray with the mini cocktail glasses garnished with lime slices. Make another pitcher of mojitos and have it ready in the refrigerator for the next round. Enjoy !

Orange or Pineapple Mojito

For an orange or pineapple mojito, replace lime juice with orange or pineapple juice. Use orange or pineapple pieces instead of the lime chunks. Then continue with the rest of the recipe. Enjoy !

Caipirinha (ki per rin ya) Cocktail from Brazil

This traditional lime cocktail originated in Brazil. It uses a very traditional Brazilian sugar cane liqueur called Cachuca. You can find Cachuca at your favorite liquor store. It is sometimes hard to find but most stores will carry at least one variety of Cachuca. You can use a light rum as a good substitute.

You will need 10 -12 small mini cocktail glass and a small 40-50 oz glass pitcher.

10 oz Cachuca or light rum
3-4 fresh limes, chunked
10 sugar cubes
12 oz lemon lime soda or club soda
Some crushed ice
10 lime slices for garnish

In the bottom of the glass pitcher, crush the sugar cubes and the fresh lime chunks together. Add the Cachuca and soda. Add crushed ice and stir. Serve on a tray with mini cocktail glasses garnished with lime slices. I like to serve Caipirinhas with a delicious appetizer of mango salsa and shrimp. Enjoy !

Peruvian Pisco Sour

This traditional lime cocktail originated in southern Peru. It uses a very traditional Peruvian colorless brandy made from grapes called Pisco. If you can not find Pisco at your favorite liquor store, you can use a light rum as a substitute. But Pisco is what makes this cocktail unique and delicious. My friends from Peru told me it is traditionally served in a double old fashion glass or a casual wine glass. But for a tasting party, I like to serve it in a small cordial or tasting shooter.

You will need 10 -12 small mini cocktail glasses and a small 40-50 oz glass pitcher.

10 oz Pisco or light rum
10 oz fresh lime juice
12 oz lemon lime soda or club soda
2 oz Angostura Bitters
Some crushed ice
2-3 limes, chunked for garnish

In a glass pitcher, add fresh lime juice, Pisco and the soda. Add crushed ice and stir. Top off with the Angostura Bitters if desired. Serve on a tray with mini cocktail glasses garnished with several lime chunks in each glass. Serve with your favorite Peruvian appetizer. Enjoy !

Pina Colada

Making Pina Coladas is almost as much fun as drinking them. They are so related to the tropics and summer parties. Pineapple, coconut and maraschino cherries all mixed together is just what everyone needs for a summer pick me up. I love serving them in these mini brandy glasses because they look like miniature coconuts when filled. This recipe will make a generous pitcher full for everyone to enjoy.

You will need a blender, a 40-50 oz glass pitcher and 10 -12 mini cocktail glasses.

3 oz light rum
6 oz pineapple juice
4 oz coconut milk
1/2 cup fresh or canned pineapple chunks
2-3 cups crushed ice

10 -12 maraschino cherries and a couple of slices of fresh pineapple for garnish

When you are short on time, and many of us are when putting together a tasting party, a store-purchased Pina Colada mix will work as a good substitute.

In a blender, add the first four ingredients. Blend until smooth. Add the crushed ice and blend until frothy. Pour into a glass pitcher or serve right from the blender. Garnish all your small cocktail glasses with the pineapple wedge and maraschino cherry on a toothpick. Serve it at a tasting party with some fresh grilled chicken kabobs with teriyaki sauce and a mixed green salad. Enjoy !

Brazilian Carnival Batidas

This is the traditional cocktail of carnival. During the whole week before Lent, millions of Brazilians party all over the country. This is carnival. People dance, sing, eat and drink Batidas, a potent alcoholic smoothie and traditionally made with the Brazilian liqueur called Cachuca; you can also substitute rum, white wine or champagne if you can not find Cachuca at your local liquor store. But if you want a festive and traditional party like the Brazilians, you have to have the real thing. I make a blender full of these and serve them in any fun little cocktail glass.

2 cups of tropical fruit (pineapple, mango, oranges, limes, melon, strawberries, etc.)
1 cup whole milk
3 tbsp sugar
1/2 cup Cachuca or light rum
4 tbsp fresh lime juice
Dash of salt

4 cups crushed ice
a lime wedge and granulated sugar for rim garnish

Place the first six ingredients in a blender and blend until smooth. Add the crushed ice and blend until frothy, about one minute. Place the granulated sugar in a saucer. Rub the lime wedge around the rim of each glass and dip the glass into the sugar to coat the rim. Place all the small cocktail glasses on a tray and serve with a pitcher or blender full of refreshing Batidas. Some homemade mango salsa and chips is a delicious appetizer when served with Brazilian Batidas. Enjoy !

Classic Red Sangria

Nothing is more refreshing and tasty than a pitcher full of freshly made Sangria. It was originally made in Spain and Mexico with all the left over ripe tropical fruit one would have in the kitchen. The riper the fruit the better. They would toss it in a large glass jug with some table wine and let it sit for days. There are many variations of Sangria and any fruit combination is possible. Be sure to make this recipe a few hours in advance so the fruit can work with the wine. I make a pitcherful and serve it in mini wine tasting glasses or short clunky rocks glass for that old world effect.

You will need a small glass pitcher and 10 -12 mini cocktail glasses

One bottle dark, robust red wine
4 oz brandy or Cointreau or Grand Marnier, optional but needed
one whole orange, lime and lemon, sliced
1/2 cup orange juice
1/2 cup sliced strawberries
1/2 cup fresh raspberries
1/2 cup fresh blueberries
1 peach, sliced
1 tbsp sugar
12 oz club soda, lemon lime juice or ginger ale
2 cups ice

Place the first nine ingredients in a pitcher a few hours or so before serving. A little before serving add the soda and ice and let chill. The brandy is optional but really adds a richness and depth to the drink. You can make Sangria with almost any combination of fresh fruit. Sometimes I only use citrus fruits or all fresh berries. Sangria is wonderful when served with small tasting appetizers and desserts. Enjoy !

White Wine Sangria

Sangria is one of those hidden or forgotten treasures in the cocktail world. Whether it's a red and white sangria, there is nothing more refreshing and tasty than a pitcher full of freshly made Sangria. There are many variations of Sangria and any fruit combination is possible. Be sure to make this recipe a few hours in advance so the fruit can work with the wine. I make a pitcherful and serve it in mini wine tasting glasses or a short chunky rocks glasses. Either one will add a festive flair to your next cocktail party.

You will need a small glass pitcher and 10 -12 mini cocktail glasses.

One bottle white wine, like Chardonnay or Pinot Grigio
3-4 oz brandy or Cointreau or Grand Marnier, optional
One whole, orange, lime and lemon, sliced
2 peaches, sliced
1 tbsp sugar
12 oz club soda or lemon lime soda
2 cups ice

Place the first five ingredients in a pitcher an hour or so before serving. A little before serving add the soda and ice and let chill. The brandy is optional but really adds a richness and depth to the Sangria. You can make Sangria with almost any combination of fresh fruit. Sometimes I will only use citrus fruits or all fresh melons. Try using only fresh, very ripe peaches when they are in season. Sangria is wonderful when served with small tasting appetizers and desserts. Enjoy !

Tropical Tequila Sunset

Nothing screams "I want to be on vacation in the Caribbean" more than a Tequila Sunset. Refreshing and delicious. You can make a pitcher of these but they look a lot more festive when you make them individually, because of the layering effects. I serve them along with some pina coladas, served in a tall skinny mini glass with a lot of tasting appetizers right when we all get back from a day at the beach. They are just perfect for that hour or so of cool down and relaxing with friends.

You will need a small glass 40-50 oz pitcher and 10 -12 mini cocktail glasses.

For a pitcher:
12 oz tequila
24 oz orange juice
1 oz Grenadine
Crushed ice

Single serving:
1 oz tequila
2 oz orange juice
Dash of grenadine
Crushed ice

12 orange slices and 12 maraschino cherries for garnish

When making it in a pitcher, combine all ingredients and stir slightly. For individual servings, pour a shot of tequila in the glass over the crushed ice. Fill with orange juice and stir. Carefully add a dash or so of Grenadine down the side of the glass. Do not mix or stir. Garnish with an orange slice and cherry. Add a straw. It is that quick and simple but so delicious. Enjoy !

Classic Cocktails

Midtown Manhattan

A pitcher full of Manhattans is about as classic as Lauren Bacall and Humphrey Bogart sitting on a veranda in Hollywood (or today it would be Brad Pitt and Angelina Jolie sitting on a beach in Croatia). Manhattans are robust and over the top with the fullness of rich, age old whiskey. They can be made sweet or dry, depending on the type of vermouth you use. A Perfect Manhattan is made with equal parts of sweet and dry vermouth.

You will need a small sleek glass pitcher and 8-10 mini cocktail glasses

12 oz Canadian Whiskey
6 oz vermouth (sweet or dry)
1 oz Augostura Bitters
2 cups ice

12 maraschino cherries
12 lemon twists for garnish

Mix the first three ingredients together in a pitcher full of ice. Stir. Then strain into the mini martini or cocktail glasses and garnish with a cherry and lemon twist. Quick, simple and perfect. Enjoy !

Bloody Mary

What could be more traditional for a morning brunch than a big batch of Bloody Marys? I've also added a non alcoholic version for those who just want the delicious and refreshing tastes of tomato juice and spices. This looks great when served in a tall skinny glass with a stalk of fresh celery.

You will need a small 40-50 oz glass pitcher and 8 -10 mini cocktail glasses

12 oz vodka
24 oz tomato or V-8 juice
2 oz lemon juice
1 tbsp of Tabasco Sauce
1 tsp of Worcestershire sauce
Salt and pepper
12 sticks of celery for garnish
Some ice cubes

In a pitcher, add the tomato juice, lemon juice, Tabasco and Worcestershire sauce. Add salt and pepper to taste. Add vodka and ice cubes. Stir well. Place pitcher on a tray with several tall skinny glasses garnished with a celery stick. Enjoy !

For something a little different, try substituting the vodka with Tequila or Light Rum or Gin.

Virgin Mary

A very simple solution, follow the recipe from above but leave out the vodka. Enjoy !

John or Tom Collins

This is as old as time and about as special as they come. Tom Collins has been around since the silent movies (that's around 1930's for you younger folks). They are light and refreshing. A pitcher of Tom Collins is sure to pick up the tempo of any tasting party.

You will need a small 40-50 oz glass pitcher and 10 -12 mini cocktail glasses

8 oz gin
4 oz lemon juice
2 tbsp granulated sugar
2 cups of crushed ice
12 oz club soda or lemon lime soda

10 lemon slices and 10 maraschino cherries for garnish

Combine first five ingredients in a glass pitcher and stir until sugar is dissolved. Serve the pitcher of Tom Collins on a tray with tall glasses garnished with a lemon slice and maraschino cherries. You can make these ahead or serve the pitcher on a tray and let your guests help themselves. Either way, your guests will love these. Enjoy !

To make a John Collins, substitute a good bourbon for the gin. Follow the rest of the recipe from above. Enjoy !

Strawberry Daiquiri

The Daiquiri has been around forever. Making it with strawberries, frothy and frozen, just puts it over the top. I sometimes add a couple of raspberries or blueberries to jazz it up. Either way, original or jazzed up, its refreshingly delicious. You can serve it in almost any mini tasting cocktail glass but I like to use the mini wine or cordial glass. It just makes it all the more special.

You will need a blender, a 40-50 oz glass pitcher and 10 -12 mini cocktail glasses

12 oz light rum
4 oz strawberry liqueur or cocktail mix
2 oz lime juice
1 oz orange juice
1 oz simple syrup (see page 14)
12 fresh strawberries, very ripe
some crushed ice
10 -12 fresh strawberries for garnish

In a blender, place the first six ingredients and blend until smooth. Add the crushed ice and blend until frothy and almost frozen. Serve in a glass pitcher or right out of the blender. Garnish the mini cocktail glasses with fresh strawberries and place on a beautiful tray to serve. Enjoy !

Sexy.com

Wow ! This is an incredibly smooth and refreshing cocktail that will really wake up your appetite. It has a sexy blue color that really fits into the next generation. You need to serve it in a glass shape that is sleek and sexy. These are great served in a small glass pitcher or made in a shaker and served.

You will need a small 40 oz glass pitcher and 8 -10 mini cocktail glasses

8 oz of a good quality vodka
8 oz Blue Curacao
8 oz lemonade
1 oz simple syrup (see page 14)
2 cups crushed ice

30 maraschino cherries, 3 per toothpick

Pour the first four ingredients in a glass pitcher filled with crushed ice, stir slightly and serve. Garnish with a toothpick full of maraschino cherries. Enjoy !

Mango Bellini

This is not actually a traditional cocktail but it looks and tastes as good as any in this chapter. It is great served for brunch. I love to serve this cocktail in a tall skinny glass because of the champagne and sparkling bubbles. I've also made this with ordinary orange juice or pineapple juice for something different or when I cannot find the mango-orange juice.

You will need a small glass pitcher and 10 -12 mini cocktail glasses

12 oz cold mango juice or orange mango or pineapple juice
Bottle of chilled champagne
10 slices of fresh mango or orange for garnish

A few ice cubes

Fill a glass pitcher about half full of any juice you prefer. Add the chilled champagne and stir. Add a few ice cubes to keep it cold. Serve on a tray or platter along with your tall skinny glasses garnished with either mango or orange slices. Enjoy !

Long Island Iced Tea

Long Island Iced Teas go back a few years but for today's tasting parties they are perfect when made in a small glass pitcher and served in tall skinny glasses with tropical fruit for garnish. This is a very potent cocktail, even when served in a mini glass. Make sure you have lots of tasting appetizers available.

Start with a small 40-50 oz glass pitcher and 8 -10 mini cocktail glasses

4 oz Cointreau
4 oz gin
4 oz vodka
4 oz white rum
4 oz tequila
2 oz fresh lime juice
2 oz simple syrup (optional)
12 oz can of cola, chilled
1 cup of ice
Several orange, lime and lemon slices for garnish

Plus one ice bucket full of ice used for serving

Put a few ice cubes in the glass pitcher. Add all the liquor and lime juice. Stir gently. Add the cola and stir again. I don't add a lot of ice in the pitcher. It tends to dilute the cocktail at a tasting party. Have an ice bucket full of ice cubes or crushed ice available for your guests to fill their individual mini glasses as needed. Garnish with some citrus slices and you are ready to go. Serve with your favorite appetizers and Enjoy !

Party Punches

Tropical Punch

Party punches have always had the stigma that they were for little old grey haired ladies. Well, think again. Today's party punches have pizzazz and are great for when you need to serve a lot of people at one time. Make two or three different kinds. You don't always need three punch bowls. Use a big, deep serving bowl or a big container. For a tasting party, I use 80-90 oz pitchers. When you're outside, use a big soup pot. Dress it up by wrapping the handles with colorful napkins. Tropical Punch is one of my favorites because it is refreshing and not real sweet, so the guys will also like it.

This will make enough to fill a large 90 oz glass pitcher. You may need to adjust the quantities of the ingredients to fit the size of your container.

2 liters club soda or ginger ale or lemon lime soda
1 bottle white wine or 8 oz vodka or light rum
1 cup orange juice
1/4 cup lime juice
One orange, one lemon, one lime, sliced
3-4 slices of fresh pineapple
2 mangos, peeled and chunked
Any additional fresh fruit you like
4 cups ice cubes

Several sliced oranges, lemon or limes for garnish, jar of maraschino cherries and some toothpicks, optional

Put all the fresh fruit in the bottom of your glass pitcher or punch bowl. Add the soda and whatever alcoholic beverage you want to add. Add the ice and stir carefully. I use a slice of fruit and a cherry on a toothpick and put it inside all my punch glasses on a serving tray. Serve and Enjoy !

White Wedding Punch

A very simple but elegant White Wedding Punch. It's delicious and refreshing and will go a long way when you have a lot of people to serve. It is great for bridal showers and outdoor weddings.

This will make enough to fill a large glass punch bowl. You may need to adjust the quantities of the ingredients to fit the size of your container if you are making the punch for a tasting party. You can use any light colored alcoholic beverage: champagne, white wine, vodka, gin or a light rum. I use champagne because it is for a wedding.

4 liters of cold club soda or lemon lime soda (club soda will make it more tart)
2 bottles of Champagne, chilled
One lemon, sliced
4 cups ice cubes or crushed ice

You can garnish this punch with almost anything, but traditionally, it is served plain in a very tall skinny flute glass or a beautiful mini punch cup for a tasting party.

Fill your punch bowl with the cool soda. Be careful not to put ice cold beverages in a warm punch bowl. Thermal shock could break the glass bowl. Carefully add the champagne. Add the ice and stir. Garnish with a few slices of lemon. Serve and Enjoy !

Holiday Punch

Holiday Punch will add a lot of pizzazz to any party and is great for when you need to serve a lot of people at one time. For a little holiday decoration, place your punch bowl in the center of an evergreen ring or wreath. Try putting it on a silver platter filled with Christmas ornaments or pine cones.

This recipe will make enough to fill a large punch bowl. You may need to adjust the quantities of the ingredients to fit the size of your container. Use white wine or vodka if you don't want a red punch to spill and stain your carpeting. I love to use red during the holidays, because it's so traditional and adds a real feeling of family and being together.

For a tasting party, use a 90 oz glass pitcher and divide the recipe in half, make one with alcohol and one without.

4 liters of club soda or ginger ale or lemon lime soda
2 bottles of dark red wine, like a Merlot or Cabernet
3 cups cranberry juice
One orange, one lemon, one lime, sliced
Handful of fresh cranberries, raspberries and blueberries
4 cups ice cubes

Several oranges, lemon or limes for garnish, jar of maraschino cherries and some toothpicks, optional

Put all the fresh fruit in the bottom of your punch bowl. Add the soda and whatever alcoholic beverage you want to add. Add the ice and stir carefully. I take a slice of fruit and a cherry on a toothpick and put one inside each of my punch glasses and arrange on a silver tray or all around the punch bowl. Serve along with your favorite tasting appetizers. Enjoy !

Summer Mojito Punch

Definitely one of my favorite summer punches, because I love the taste of mint, lime and rum. Or maybe because it is so light and refreshing. I freeze a small ring of ice and lime slices and float it in the center of my punch bowl and then fill the ring with sprigs of fresh mint. It looks fabulous.

This recipe will make enough to fill a large punch bowl. You may need to adjust the quantities of the ingredients to fit the size of your container. For a tasting party, I use a large glass pitcher and 10 -12 mini cocktail glasses.

2 liters of cold club soda or lemon lime soda
8 oz light rum
5-6 fresh limes, chunked
1/2 cup lime juice
20 sugar cubes
Large bunch of fresh mint, about 1/2 cup
3-4 fresh limes, sliced for garnish
8 cups crushed ice

In the bottom of your punch bowl, add the sugar cubes, lime chunks, lime juice and half the fresh mint (about 1/4 cup of mint leaves) Crush or muddle all together until the sugar is dissolved. Carefully add the soda, crushed ice and light rum and stir. Add the lime slices to the top of the punch bowl or use them for garnish in each mini cocktail glass. Add the ice ring filled with fresh mint. Serve and Enjoy !

Smoothie & Non Alcoholic Cocktails

Strawberry Banana Power Smoothie

Smoothies are great anytime of the year. They can be healthy or not so, depending on whether you add a little alcohol to the recipe. Either way, they are delicious. I make my smoothies in a blender so they are frothy and smooth.

All these smoothie recipes can be made with or without alcohol. They can also be made with ice cream, yogurt or fresh milk. It all depends on how rich or healthy you want them to be.

You will need a blender, a small glass 30-40 oz pitcher and 10 -12 mini cocktail glasses.

2 cups vanilla yogurt or ice cream
2 cups fresh or frozen strawberries
4 oz light rum or vodka
2 bananas, sliced
1/2 cup orange juice

2 cups crushed ice
One orange, sliced or 5-6 fresh strawberries cut in half for garnish, optional

Start with a clean blender. Add the first five ingredients and turn your blender on high for 15-20 seconds. This will depend on how powerful your blender is. It may take a few more seconds to get everything pureed and smooth. Add the crushed ice and blend until frothy. Pour into a glass pitcher or serve right from the blender. I serve the smoothies in tall, skinny mini cocktail glass and arrange them on a tray. I garnish with a orange slice or fresh strawberry. Serve and Enjoy !

Tropical Mango Smoothie

This smoothie is a delicious combination of mango and pineapple. I've added a little light rum or vodka to jazz it up. This also makes it an adult beverage and not really a smoothie anymore. I make it in a blender so it is smooth and frothy. You can leave out the alcohol for the little ones. This makes a great cocktail for a tasting party or morning brunch.

You will need a blender, a small glass pitcher and 8-10 mini cocktail glasses for serving.

2 cups vanilla yogurt or ice cream
1 cup fresh mango, peeled and chopped
1 cup fresh or canned pineapple
4 oz light rum or vodka (optional)
1 cup orange juice
2 cups crushed ice

8 -10 pieces of fresh pineapple or orange slices for garnish

Start with a clean blender. Add all the ingredients and turn your blender on high for 15-20 seconds. This will depend on how powerful your blender is. It may take a few more seconds to get everything pureed and smooth. Serve in tall, skinny glasses on a tray. Garnish with a slice of fresh pineapple or orange slice on the edge of the glass. Serve and Enjoy !

Berry Berry Smoothie

This is another delicious smoothie that is great anytime of the year. I always make my smoothies in a blender so they are frothy and smooth. As mentioned earlier, you can add vodka or rum to make this an adult beverage. It is really great either way.

Berry Berry Smoothies can also be made with ice cream, yogurt or fresh milk. It all depends on how rich or healthy you want to make them.

You will need a blender, a glass pitcher and 8 -10 mini cocktail glasses for serving.

2 cups vanilla yogurt or ice cream
2 cups fresh or frozen strawberries
1 cup raspberries
1 cup fresh or frozen blueberries
1 cup of blackberries
1/2 cup orange juice

2 cups crushed ice
1 cup of fresh berries for garnish and toothpicks

Start with a clean blender. Add the first six ingredients and turn your blender on high for 15-20 seconds. This will depend on how powerful your blender is. It may take a few more seconds to get everything pureed and smooth. Add the crushed ice and blend until frothy. Serve in tall, skinny glasses on a tray. I garnish with a toothpick full of fresh berries. Serve and Enjoy !

Citrus Orange Smoothie

This has traditionally been called an "Orange Julius" but I am adding a different twist by adding tangerine and peaches. If you want this a little less sweet, use plain yogurt instead of vanilla. Either way, it is delicious.

You will need a blender, a 40-50 oz glass pitcher and 8 -10 mini cocktail glasses.

2 cups orange juice
1 orange, peeled and seeds removed
1 tangerine, peeled and seeds removed
1 cup canned or fresh peaches, sliced
2 cups vanilla yogurt

2 cups crushed ice
12 orange slices for garnish, optional

Process the first five ingredients in a blender until smooth. Add the crushed ice and process until smooth and frothy. Pour into a glass pitcher or serve right out of the blender. Serve in a fancy mini cocktail glass with a orange slice for garnish. Enjoy !

Citrus Orange Rum Smoothie

To make this an adult beverage, add 6 oz of light rum or vodka when you are adding the crushed ice from the recipe above. Follow the rest of the instructions. Serve and Enjoy !

Cranberry Cocktail

This is very refreshing and is something I order all the time when I'm traveling and when everyone else at the bar is ordering a beer or martini. They always ask, Oh! What are you drinking? I simply say, "A Cranberry Cocktail." It will really quench your thirst and you can also be the designated driver. It is really great at a tasting party. It has just a few simple ingredients but looks great.

You will need a 40 oz glass pitcher and 10 -12 mini cocktail glasses.

16 oz cranberry juice
16 oz ginger ale or lemon lime soda
2 oz lime juice
1 cup of crushed ice
12 lime or orange slices for garnish

For an added twist, add 1/4 cup orange juice

In a small glass pitcher, add the first four ingredients and stir. Place a lime or orange slice in each cocktail glass for garnish. Place the pitcher of Cranberry Cocktails on a tray with the mini glassware and serve. Enjoy !

Mad Maxx Cocktail

I made this tasty cocktail to appeal to all the guys out there who were looking for something a little more on the cutting edge. Fortunately, the gals love it too. It tastes as sleek and refreshing as it looks. This needs to be served in a cool, sleek looking glass tumbler garnished with several fruit wedges and a maraschino cherry.

I like making this cocktail in a small glass pitcher, about 40-50 oz and 8 -10 mini cocktail glasses for serving.

8 oz blue raspberry cocktail mix
16 oz lemon lime soda, cold
1 oz lime juice

Some ice cubes
Some orange and lime slices for garnish
Several mint leaves for garnish (optional)

For a wonderful alcoholic cocktail, add 6 oz vodka or light rum

Mix all ingredients together in a pitcher. Have an ice bucket full of ice available. When serving on a tasting buffet, line the glasses up and add a few citrus wedges to each glass. Let your guests add their own ice and fill the glasses with some Mad Maxx. This cocktail looks great in almost any sleek mini glass tumbler or stem. Serve and Enjoy !

Britney Bang (formerly a Shirley Temple)

What would be more appropriate for today's consumer than to rename America's most popular kiddy cocktail after a trendy Hollywood starlet? It's still the same delicious non alcoholic drink it's always been, but with a new twist. I love to serve it in the little mini brandy stem because it is so darn cute. This cocktail works great at a family party when served in mini cocktails glasses. The kids will really feel important and will just love you.

You will need a small 40-50 oz glass pitcher and 8 -10 mini cocktail glasses for serving.

12 oz cranberry juice
12 oz orange, grapefruit or pineapple juice
12 oz lemon lime soda
some ice cubes
8 -10 maraschino cherries, several orange slices, one for each glass for garnish

Place all the ingredients in the glass pitcher with several ice cubes. Garnish each glass with a orange slice and maraschino cherry.

To make this a wonderful adult beverage, try adding 4 oz vodka or light rum. It's pretty tasty either way. Serve and Enjoy !

Coffees, Teas and Hot Chocolates

Irish Coffee

Fresh brewed coffee combines well with alcohol. Probably two of our greatest vices. Perhaps the best known version is the delicious blend of Irish Whiskey and fresh brewed coffee, better known world wide as an Irish Coffee. It is ideally served as an after dinner drink, but is really good almost anytime. Made famous in San Francisco at the Buena Vista on Fisherman's Wharf.

You will need an insulated coffee thermos or carafe to keep this hot when serving it on your tasting party buffet and 8 -10 mini Irish coffee mugs.

12 oz of any good Irish Whiskey
6 cups of freshly brewed strong robust coffee
6 tsp sugar

Some whipped topping or whipping cream

Ideally, I like to serve this as soon as the fresh coffee is brewed. I make them up all at one time and serve them to my guests. But if you are serving it at a tasting party, store the coffee mixed with the sugar in an insulated thermos or carafe. Add the Irish Whiskey as it is served. Sometimes I pour it into a small wine carafe on the table next to the coffee carafe. Have a bowl of the whipped topping on the table so your guests can add it to their Irish coffee if they want to make it rich and delicious. Serve this with your favorite mini desserts. Enjoy !

Bailey's & Cream Cappuccino

Cappuccinos are best made in an espresso machine but this recipe is really delicious and pretty simple to make at home with regular fresh brewed coffee and just a few simple ingredients and standard everyday kitchen utensils.

Ideally, you'll need to serve these delicious mini cappuccinos immediately when everything is hot and fresh. You will need a blender or electric mixer. This recipe is a little easier and ideal for a tasting party. You'll need a 24 oz insulated server or carafe and 8 -10 mini Irish coffee mugs.

4 cups of very strong, freshly brewed Italian roasted coffee
4 oz creme de cocoa
3 oz Baileys Irish Cream Liqueur
1 oz amaretto
3 tsp sugar
2 cups whole milk
8 oz whipped topping
2 oz chocolate shavings

Heat the milk in a saucepan over low heat until it almost boils. Use a hand electric mixer and mix on high for a minute or so until frothy. Combine the Irish Cream Liqueur, creme de cocoa and amaretto, sugar and the fresh brewed coffee. Pour the coffee mixture into the insulated carafe. Add the steamed milk to the carafe and stir. Have a container of whipped topping and a small bowl with the chocolate shavings on a small tray along with the coffee carafe so your guests can help themselves to a wonderful tasting party cappuccino. Serve and Enjoy !

Mocha Rum Latte

Lattes are simply large cups of delicious roasted coffee with a lot of milk. This particular latte has all that and a little rum to jazz it up. Sometimes I even use a spiced rum to really add some pizzazz. Serving it in little mini mugs just makes it all the more special.

You will need a 24 oz insulated coffee carafe and 6 - 8 mini coffee mugs for a festive tasting party.

2 cups freshly brewed strong black coffee
1 cup whole milk
4 oz chocolate syrup
4 oz light or spiced rum (optional) more or less depending on your tastes

8 oz whipped topping for garnish

In a small saucepan, bring the milk to a soft boil over low heat. This will take a few minutes. Remove from the heat and whisk a few minutes until frothy. Add the rum and chocolate syrup to your hot coffee and pour it into the insulated carafe. Slowly pour the steamed milk into the carafe and stir. On a festive tray, place the carafe and a glass bowl of whipped topping. Let your guests help themselves. You could also have some chocolate shavings or cinnamon sprinkles in a small bowl for additional garnishes.

Serve your Mocha Rum Lattes with several mini desserts and any delicious little fancy cookie. Serve and Enjoy !

Spiced Tea

Spiced tea is ideal for a tasting party, especially later in the evening. Teas are especially trendy right now and an ideal alternative to coffee. You'll need an insulated carafe or heavy ceramic tea pot for serving at a tasting party.

You could use various loose leaf spiced teas or when you are in a hurry, use 2 Constant Comment tea bags and one orange spice tea bag as a good substitute. You will need 8 -10 mini mugs for serving.

6 cups cold water
1 tsp whole cloves
1 cinnamon stick
3/4 c orange juice
2 tbsp lemon juice
1/2 c sugar
3 tbsp loose black tea
Several cinnamon sticks for garnish, optional

In a stainless steel saucepan, add water, orange juice, lemon juice, sugar, whole cloves and cinnamon stick and bring almost to a boil. Remove from heat and add black tea and let steep for 5 minutes. Strain the tea leaves and spices. Pour the tea mixture into a insulated carafe or large tea pot. To keep your tea hot at your tasting party, preheat the carafe or tea pot with boiling water. Empty the hot water before adding the fresh brewed spiced tea. Serve in mini coffee mugs or mini footed Irish coffees. Enjoy !

For a refreshing twist in the summer, serve the spiced tea over a glass full of ice. Garnish with an orange slice and fresh mint. Serve and Enjoy !

Killer Hot Chocolate

Hot Chocolate (or Hot Cocoa as many of us call it) is soothing and comforting and really delicious when you need something to warm you up. It is ideal for a late night tasting party when you need something hot to finish off the evening. Several mini mugs just make this hot drink all the more special.

You will need a small insulated carafe to keep this hot for a few hours during the evening or at your tasting party. You will also need 8 -10 mini mugs for serving.

1/2 cup of dry cocoa
1/2 c sugar
1/3 cup water
4 cups whole milk
3/4 tsp vanilla
Dash of salt

1 oz sweet chocolate, shaved or some chocolate syrup, optional
1 cup whipped topping or miniature marshmallows, for garnish, optional

Combine the dry cocoa, sugar, salt and water in a saucepan. Stir over medium heat until chocolate melts completely. Gradually stir in milk and vanilla. Heat slowly, do not boil. Beat with mixer on medium speed for two minutes. Pour into insulated server or serve immediately in mini coffee mugs. Top with miniature marshmallows or whipped topping and drizzle with chocolate syrup or chocolate shavings. Serve and Enjoy !

Belgium Cocoa

Belgium Cocoa is rich, dark and creamy and is just about as close to heaven as you can get. If you like dark chocolate, you will love Belgium Cocoa. Serving it in mini mugs makes it all the more special. This is wonderful served with small shortbread cookies.

You will need a 24 oz insulated coffee server if you are having a tasting party and 8 -10 mini Irish coffee mugs for serving.

4 ounces unsweetened dark chocolate
1/2 cup sugar
Dash of salt
1/2 cup water
1/4 tsp vanilla
3 cups milk

If using sweetened dark chocolate, omit the sugar

8 oz of whipped topping
1 ounce dark chocolate, shaved for garnish

Combine the dark chocolate squares, sugar, salt and water in a saucepan. Stir over low heat until chocolate melts completely. Gradually stir in milk and vanilla. Heat slowly until it almosts boils. Beat with mixer on medium speed for two minutes. Pour into insulated server or serve immediately in mini coffee mugs. Top with whipped topping and shaved chocolate and serve. Enjoy !

Beer and Wine Tastings

Beer Tastings

Beer Tastings is for a special occasion when you want your guests to sample a variety of different beers from various brewers. Today, craft beers are available at almost any high end grocery or liquor store. More and more retailers are carrying a larger variety of craft beers from all over the world. In the United States, it is the fastest growing adult beverage category. You'll need several different craft beers. I suggest several different light pilsners and darker beers like porters and stouts. Always start your beer tastings evening with lighter beers and end with darker beers.

A simple golden rule about serving craft beers: Lighter beers are normally served cold and darker beers are served slightly chilled or at room temperature. But be sure to look at the carton or bottle, as some newer craft beers have different guide lines.

Many different beer glasses and mugs are available to help you experience the fullest tasting experience possible. I've used several different mini beer tasters because they are small enough to give each of your guests a small taste of each of these craft beers. Narrower glasses are best for lighter pilsners and wider glasses are best suited for darker craft beers.

Be sure to serve your favorite craft brews with some delicious tasting appetizers. There are many books available that explain the right food to serve with your favorite craft or specialty brews.

Having a craft beer tasting party is a great way to bring friends and family together for something a little different and a unique way to try many different types of craft beer from all over the world, especially when served with multiple tasting appetizers.

Wine Tastings

Wine tasting is something that can turn a relatively ordinary party into a very special and festive cocktail party. All you need to make this special is several different types of wine. I would start with two or three bottles of white and the same with reds. It all depends on the number of guests you've invited to your party. Equally as important is having several small wine tasting glasses, usually 3 - 4 ounces each, originally called cordial or sherry stems. They work perfectly for wine tastings.

Also ask your local wine connoisseur about what cheese and chocolates to serve with different wines. Having a wine tasting party should always include some delicious appetizers and cheeses to compliment the wines. And it is just plain smart.

A few tips on serving wine: White wine is usually served chilled at around 40-45 degrees and red wine should be served at room temperature. There is another simple temperature rule. White wine should be chilled and then removed from the refrigerator 20 minutes before serving. Red wine should be at room temperature and chilled 20 minutes before serving.

Check with your local wine store and ask the sommelier about food pairings. There are many fine red wines that go wonderfully with chocolates and fruity desserts. Those same red or white wines are fantastic with various cheeses and fresh fruits. There has always been one simple rule about pairing food and wine: It has been said red meats, red wines and white meats and fish with white wines. Some say that is old fashioned, because today you eat and drink what appeals to you and your guests.

My rule has always been "Select a wine that you enjoy and are comfortable with, whether it is red or white and eat what you enjoy."

INDEX

BEER TASTINGS   120

CLASSIC COCKTAILS
        Bloody Mary   66
        John or Tom Collins   68
        Long Island Iced Tea   76
        Mango Bellini   74
        Midtown Mahattan   64
        Sexy.com   72
        Strawberry Daiquiri   70
        Whiskey Sour   70

COFFEES
        Bailey's & Cream Cappuccino   108
        Irish Coffee   106
        Mocha Rum Latte   110

HOT CHOCOLATE
        Belgium Cocoa   116
        Killer Hot Chocolate   114

MARGARITAS
        Classic Margarita   38
        Citrus Orange Margarita   40
        Strawberry Margarita   42

MARTINIS
        Appletini   26
        Cosmopolitan   22
        Chocolate Martini   24
        Chocolate Mocha Martini   24
        Classic or Dirty Martini   30
        Cotton Candy Martini   34
        Lemontini   28
        Mojotini   32
        Pomegranate Martini   36
        Pineapple Martini   28

NON-ALCOHOLIC COCKTAILS

Britney Bang (formerly a Shirley Temple)	102
Cranberry Cocktail	98
Mad Maxx	100

PARTY PUNCHES

Holiday Party Punch	84
Summer Mojito Punch	86
Tropical Punch	80
White Wedding Punch	82

SMOOTHIES

Berry Berry	94
Orange Citrus	96
Orange Rum Citrus	96
Strawberry Banana	90
Tropical Mango	92

TEAS

Spiced Tea	112

TROPICAL COCKTAILS

Brazilian Carnival Batidas	54
Ciapirinha	48
Classic Red Sangria	56
Mojito Mojito	46
Orange or Pineapple Mojito	46
Pina Colada	52
Peruvian Pisco Sour	50
Singapore Sling	92
Tropical Tequila Sunset	60
White Wine Sangria	58

WINE TASTINGS   122

About the author.

This is ROBERT ZOLLWEG's third cookbook on **Just Tastings**. His first cookbook was on **Just Mini Desserts**, the second on **Just Tastings** with mini appetizers, soups and salads and his third one on **Just mini Cocktails** will continue this passion. He is a native of Toledo, Ohio and has been in the tabletop industry for almost 40 years. He designs glassware, flatware and ceramic products for the retail and foodservice industry. He has worked with all of the major retailers including Crate and Barrel, Williams-Sonoma, Macy's, Pier One Imports, Cost Plus World Market, Bed Bath & Beyond, JCPenneys, Target, Kohl's, Walmart, Sears and Home Outfitters to name a few. Most of his professional career has been with Libbey Glass in Toledo, Ohio. He has traveled the world extensively looking for color and design trends and the right products to design and bring to the retail and foodservice marketplace. Robert has always had a passion for entertaining. He is also an artist-painter and works primarily with acrylic on canvas using bold primary colors. He currently lives in Toledo's Historic Old West End and in the artistic community of Saugatuck, Michigan.

To find more information about Robert Zollweg, visit his web site at www.zollwegart.com

I hope you have enjoyed my cookbook on **Just mini Cocktails**. It should help to make your next casual get together or tasting party a lot more fun and exciting.

My **Just Mini Desserts** cookbook on quick and easy mini desserts and my **Just Tastings** cookbook on appetizers, soups and salads would be a wonderful compliment to **Just mini Cocktails**. They are all available at area retailers or you can visit my web site.

www.zollwegart.com

Enjoy !

Robert

James Stevenson

Emma at the Beach

Greenwillow Books, New York

*Printed in Hong Kong
by South China Printing
Company (1988) Ltd.*

*First Edition
10 9 8 7 6 5 4 3 2 1*

*Library of Congress
Cataloging-in-Publication Data*

*Stevenson, James (date)
Emma at the beach /
James Stevenson.
p.   cm.
Summary:
Mean witches Dolores
and Lavinia torment
Emma and her
friends and retreat
to the cool comfort
of the beach,
but their victims
strike back with
a creative form
of revenge.
ISBN 0-688-08806-6.
ISBN 0-688-08807-4 (lib. bdg.)
[1. Witches—Fiction.
2. Beaches—Fiction.
3. Cartoons and comics.]
I. Title.
PZ7.S84748Eo 1990
[E]—dc19
88-34918   CIP   AC*